Cook's R...
Collecti...

C000181063

RYLAND
PETERS
& SMALL
LONDON NEW YORK

contents

introduction

This beautiful book is for everyone who loves cooking and wants to create an individual store of culinary knowledge and wisdom. Combining the advantages of a lined journal and a personal organizer, it is specially designed to allow you to retain all your treasured recipes in a safe place and make your own *Cook's Recipe Collection*. Whether you are looking for somewhere to keep your great-grandmother's advice about breadmaking or your favorite chef's ideas on using seasonal ingredients, this is the book for you.

Beginning with an invaluable section on pantry essentials, *Cook's Recipe Collection* is divided, for ease of reference, into eight tabbed sections, covering Soups & Sauces, Vegetables & Salads, Pastas, Rice & Noodles, Meat & Fish, Eggs & Cheese, Baking & Sweet Things, Party Food, and Preserves. If you categorize your recipes according to their main ingredient or characteristic, and record them in the appropriate chapter, you will be able to find what you are looking for later with a simple flick of a tab.

Illustrated by gorgeous photography and irresistibly nostalgic artworks, *Cook's Recipe Collection* includes an abundance of lined pages that you can use to make notes and write down special recipes from friends and family. Each chapter also has a pocket for storing clippings from newspapers and magazines, in addition to kitchen hints and tips handed down from generation to generation.

The Resources section starting on page 140 includes a list of useful websites and a measurements conversion chart. Add details of your own contacts on page 143.

pantry essentials

If you keep your pantry, refrigerator, and freezer well stocked, you will always be able to produce a quick meal, even if you haven't had a chance to buy anything in. In addition to basics such as pasta, rice, and beans, keep a choice of flavorings, so you can turn something ordinary into something special.

Staples

Pasta—a good variety of dried pasta, from penne or rigatoni to spaghetti or tagliatelle.

Rice—long grain, risotto, basmati, Thai jasmine or fragrant, and microwavable rice.

Egg or rice noodles—look for "straight-to-wok" brands for stir-fries.

Couscous—great for spicy dishes; simply needs plumping up in hot water or stock.

Beans—cans of cooked kidney, cannellini, and butter beans, and chickpeas.

Chopped tomatoes—canned, either plain or seasoned with mixed herbs or garlic.

Tuna flakes—canned or in jars with olive oil for salads.

Coconut milk—for Thai curries and soups.

Toasted nuts—pine nuts, almonds, hazelnuts, etc., stored in airtight containers.

Black and green olives—in jars, either plain or marinated.

Capers—jars of small capers and large caperberries for pasta, pizza, and fish dishes.

Porridge oats—for making flapjacks and desserts; choose old-fashioned rolled oats.

Taste enhancers

Sea salt flakes and freshly ground black pepper—essential seasoning.

Dark and light soy sauce—for adding salt to Asian dishes.

Thai fish sauce (nam pla)—add to all Thai food for an instant authentic flavor.

Lemon and lime juice—use instead of salt for "high" tones.

Balsamic vinegar—put in a spray bottle and spritz over salads.

Vinegars—cider, white wine, red wine, and tarragon.

Mustards—Dijon, smooth or grainy, and English mustard.

Anchovy paste or fillets—anchovy paste has a long fridge life; great for adding flavor.

Tomato paste—adds depth to tomato sauces.

Pomegranate molasses—a thick, sweet syrup for dressings.

Oils

Extra virgin olive oil—for drizzling onto salads.

Light olive oil—for cooking.

Safflower or peanut oil—for pan-frying and wok cooking.

Walnut or hazelnut oil—use in tiny amounts to add a nutty flavor to salad dressings.

Sesame oil—for seasoning Asian wok dishes; add at the end of cooking for a finishing flavor.

Seasonings & spices

Fresh ginger root—grate into Asian stir-fries and curries.

Lemongrass—chop the tender leaves and add to Thai stir-fries or curries.

Garlic—ideally, chop or crush fresh cloves, but a jar of chopped garlic can be useful.

Dried red pepper flakes—add a powerful instant heat to a wide variety of dishes; sprinkle onto steaks and fish.

Saffron threads or powder—add to marinades or mayonnaise; use sparingly or steep a pinch in hot water before adding.

Sichuan peppercorns—crush and use to coat chicken or duck breasts before cooking.

Turmeric—adds brilliant yellow color and an earthy flavor to Indian curries and vegetables.

Ground cinnamon and cinnamon sticks—good for savory or fruit desserts; stir hot chocolate with a cinnamon stick.

Pimentón (Spanish oak-smoked paprika)—spice used in chorizo sausage, good for Tex-mex flavor and barbecue sauces.

Cardamom—the outer green pod is not eaten; use in a warm fruit salad to add aromatic spice.

Cayenne pepper—adds flavor to dips and marinades.

Garam masala—added to Indian curries, toward the end of cooking, for extra flavor.

Madras curry powder—a sweet tangy base for an authentic South Indian curry.

Chinese five-spice powder—enlivens bland dishes from stir-fries to marinades.

Magic jars

Sweet chili sauce—add fresh cilantro and use as an instant dip for shrimp crackers.

Hoisin sauce—for Chinese pancakes or barbecued ribs and chicken.

Plum sauce—made from plums, apricots, and vinegar; add to pork stir-fries or use as a marinade for chicken breasts.

Good-quality mayonnaise—for quick dips and salad dressings.

Tom yum paste—an ideal base for exquisite Thai soup.

" Soup puts the heart at ease,
calms down the violence of hunger,
eliminates the tension of the day,
and awakens and refines the appetite."

Georges Auguste Escoffier

recipe

ingredients

method

source

recipe

ingredients

method

source

recipe

ingredients

method

source

recipe

ingredients

method

source

recipe

ingredients

method

source

" There is in every cook's opinion
No savory dish without an onion:
But lest your kissing should be spoiled
The onion must be thoroughly boiled."

Jonathan Swift

" To make a good salad is to be a
brilliant diplomatist—the problem
is entirely the same in both cases.
To know how much oil one must mix
with one's vinegar."

Oscar Wilde

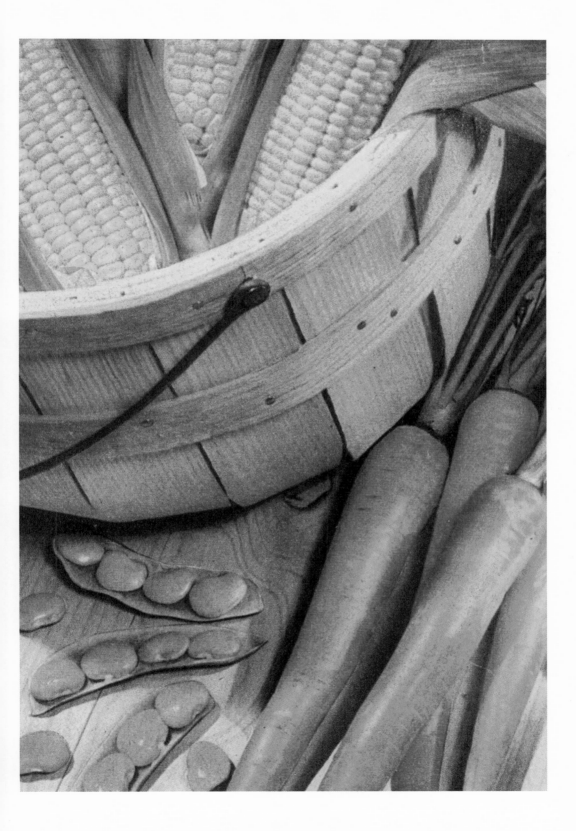

recipe

ingredients

method

source

recipe

ingredients

method

source

recipe

ingredients

method

source

recipe

ingredients

method

source

recipe

ingredients

method

source

recipe

ingredients

method

source

recipe

ingredients

method

source

recipe

ingredients

method

source

recipe

ingredients

method

source

" Rice is the best, the most
nutritive, and unquestionably the
most widespread staple in the world."

Georges Auguste Escoffier

"Everything you see
I owe to spaghetti."

Sophia Loren

recipe

ingredients

method

source

recipe

ingredients

method

source

recipe

ingredients

method

source

recipe

ingredients

method

source

recipe

ingredients

method

source

recipe

ingredients

method

source

recipe

ingredients

method

source

recipe

ingredients

method

source

recipe

ingredients

method

source

recipe

ingredients

method

source

recipe

ingredients

method

source

" Traddles cut the meat into slices; Mr. Micawber (who could do anything of this sort to perfection) covered them with pepper, mustard, salt, and cayenne; I put them on the gridiron, turned them with a fork, and took them off, under Mr. Micawber's direction; and Mrs. Micawber heated, and continually stirred, some mushroom ketchup in a little saucepan."

Charles Dickens, *David Copperfield*

recipe

ingredients

method

source

recipe

ingredients

method

source

recipe

ingredients

method

source

recipe

ingredients

method

source

recipe

ingredients

method

source

recipe

ingredients

method

source

recipe

ingredients

method

source

recipe

ingredients

method

source

recipe

ingredients

method

source

recipe

ingredients

method

source

recipe

ingredients

method

source

recipe

ingredients

method

source

recipe

ingredients

method

source

recipe

ingredients

method

source

Ways of Determining
Freshness of Eggs:
i. Hold in front of candle flame in
dark room, and the center should
look clear.
ii. Place in basin of cold water, and
they should sink.
iii. Place large end to the cheek, and
a warmth should be felt.

Fannie Farmer, *The Boston Cooking-School Cook Book*

recipe

ingredients

method

source

recipe

ingredients

method

source

recipe

ingredients

method

source

recipe

ingredients

method

source

recipe

ingredients

method

source

"I am going to learn to make bread to-morrow. So you may imagine me with my sleeves rolled up, mixing flour, milk, saleratus, etc., with a deal of grace. I advise you if you don't know how to make the staff of life to learn with dispatch."

Emily Dickinson, in a letter to a friend

"'Tis an ill cook that cannot lick his own fingers."

William Shakespeare, *Romeo and Juliet*

recipe

ingredients

method

source

recipe

ingredients

method

source

recipe

ingredients

method

source

recipe

ingredients

method

source

recipe

ingredients

method

source

recipe

ingredients

method

source

recipe

ingredients

method

source

recipe

ingredients

method

source

recipe

ingredients

method

source

recipe

ingredients

method

source

recipe

ingredients

method

source

recipe

ingredients

method

source

"The pleasures of the table belong to all ages, to all conditions, to all countries, and to every day."

Jean Anthelme Brillat-Savarin

"Strange to see how a good dinner and feasting reconciles everybody."

Samuel Pepys, *Diary*

recipe

ingredients

method

source

recipe

ingredients

method

source

recipe

ingredients

method

source

recipe

ingredients

method

source

recipe

ingredients

method

source

recipe

ingredients

method

source

"And the Quangle Wangle said
To himself on the Crumpetty Tree,—
'Jam; and Jelly; and bread;
Are the best of food for me!'"

Edward Lear, *The Quangle Wangle's Hat*

"There should always be some
flowering and maturing of the fruits
of nature in the cooking process."

Henry David Thoreau, *A Week on the Concord
and Merrimack Rivers*

recipe

ingredients

method

source

recipe

ingredients

method

source

recipe

ingredients

method

source

recipe

ingredients

method

source

recipe

ingredients

method

source

recipe

ingredients

method

source

resources

useful websites

www.ams.usda.gov/
farmersmarkets
Farmers' markets in the USA.

www.asiafoods.com
*Authentic foods from Asia
shipped all around the world.*

www.baronialimentari.it
*A wonderful selection of Italian
cheeses and groceries; orders
shipped worldwide.*

www.booksforcooks.com
*London bookshop, with cooking
classes and demonstrations.*

www.chefshop.com
*Sources the best-tasting foods
from small farmers and artisan
producers all around the world.*

www.cooking.com
*American online store selling
a wide choice of kitchenware.*

www.cookware-online.com
*A wide selection of cookware
including Jamie Oliver brand;
orders shipped worldwide.*

www.crateandbarrel.com
*Kitchen accessories and
gourmet foods.*

www.dddirect.co.uk
*Importers to the UK of fine
French foods.*

www.divertimenti.co.uk
*A comprehensive range of
kitchenware and tableware.*

www.frenchflavour.co.uk
*Specialist website selling French
food in the UK.*

www.farmersmarkets.net
*The National Association of
Farmers' Markets in the UK.*

www.globalgourmet.com
*Ingredients and recipe ideas
from all corners of the globe.*

www.greekshops.com
*Ships high-quality Greek
products around the world.*

www.igourmet.com
*One of America's leading online
gourmet food retailers.*

www.italianfooddirect.com
*Italian food and wine; orders
shipped worldwide.*

www.kitchenmarket.com
*Chiles, herbs, and spices from
around the world.*

www.mycologue
The internet mushroom store.

www.pacificrim-
gourmet.com
*Kitchenware and ingredients
from Pacific Rim countries.*

www.slowfood.com
*An international organization
that promotes food and wine
culture and defends food and
agriculture biodiversity.*

www.thecmccompany.com
*Authentic ingredients for a wide
choice of cuisines, including Far
Eastern, Chinese, and Mexican.*

www.thecookskitchen.com
*A UK site offering an enormous
selection of kitchenware.*

www.tienda.com
*A wonderful American site for
Spanish products.*

www.williams-sonoma.com
*Everything for the kitchen,
including recipes.*

conversions

Weights and measures have been rounded up
or down slightly to make measuring easier.

volume equivalents:

American	Metric	Imperial
1 teaspoon	5 ml	
1 tablespoon	15 ml	
1/4 cup	60 ml	2 fl.oz.
1/3 cup	75 ml	2 1/2 fl.oz.
1/2 cup	125 ml	4 fl.oz.
2/3 cup	150 ml	5 fl.oz. (1/4 pint)
3/4 cup	175 ml	6 fl.oz.
1 cup	250 ml	8 fl.oz.

weight equivalents:

imperial	metric
1 oz.	30 g
2 oz.	55 g
3 oz.	85 g
3 1/2 oz.	100 g
4 oz.	115 g
6 oz.	175 g
8 oz. (1/2 lb.)	225 g
9 oz.	250 g
10 oz.	280 g
12 oz.	350 g
13 oz.	375 g
14 oz.	400 g
15 oz.	425 g
16 oz. (1 lb.)	450 g

measurements:

inches	cm
1/4 inch	5 mm
1/2 inch	1 cm
1 inch	2.5 cm
2 inches	5 cm
3 inches	7 cm
4 inches	10 cm
5 inches	12 cm
6 inches	15 cm
7 inches	18 cm
8 inches	20 cm
9 inches	23 cm
10 inches	25 cm
11 inches	28 cm
12 inches	30 cm

oven temperatures:

120°C	(250°F)	Gas 1/2
140°C	(275°F)	Gas 1
150°C	(300°F)	Gas 2
170°C	(325°F)	Gas 3
180°C	(350°F)	Gas 4
190°C	(375°F)	Gas 5
200°C	(400°F)	Gas 6

measuring butter:

A US stick of butter weighs 4 oz. which is approximately
115 g or 8 tablespoons.

contacts

name..	name..
tel..	tel..
website..	website..
email...	email...
notes..	notes..
....	....
name..	name..
tel..	tel..
website..	website..
email...	email...
notes..	notes..
....	....
name..	name..
tel..	tel..
website..	website..
email...	email...
notes..	notes..
....	....
name..	name..
tel..	tel..
website..	website..
email...	email...
notes..	notes..
....	....
name..	name..
tel..	tel..
website..	website..
email...	email...
notes..	notes..
....	....
name..	name..
tel..	tel..
website..	website..
email...	email...
notes..	notes..
....	....
name..	name..
tel..	tel..
website..	website..
email...	email...
notes..	notes..
....	....

credits

Senior Editor Henrietta Heald
Designer Iona Hoyle
Picture Research Emily Westlake
Production Manager Patricia Harrington
Publishing Director Alison Starling

First published in 2007 in the UK by
Ryland Peters & Small
20–21 Jockey's Fields, London WC1R 4BW
and in the USA by
Ryland Peters & Small, Inc.
519 Broadway, 5th Floor
New York, NY 10012
www.rylandpeters.com
10 9 8 7 6 5 4 3 2 1

All rights reserved. No part of this publication may be
reproduced, stored in a retrieval system, or transmitted
in any form or by any means, electronic, mechanical,
photocopying, or otherwise, without the prior permission
of the publisher.

ISBN-10: 1-84597-494-8
ISBN-13: 978-1-84597-494-7

Printed in China.

Text and design copyright © Ryland Peters & Small 2007
Commissioned images by the following photographers
copyright © Ryland Peters & Small 2007:
Martin Brigdale, pages 4, 5, 15, 32, 37, 50, 53, 65, 72, 77,
105, 123, 144; David Brittain, page 3; Peter Cassidy, pages
6, 12, 18, 21, 27, 31, 44, 71, 80, 83, 101, 106, 111, 126, 134,
138; Jean Cazals, pages 1, 95; Nicky Dowey, page 47;
Tara Fisher, pages 93, 129; Richard Jung, page 114; Tom
Leighton, page 24; Diana Miller, page 98; David Munns,
pages 56, 90; Noel Murphy, page 142; Tham Nhu-Tran,
page 2; William Shaw, pages 9, 39; Debi Treloar, page 59;
Chris Tubbs, page 66; Polly Wreford, pages 89, 117, 141.

Images on pages 11, 23, 41, 61, 85, 97, 119, 131
reproduced courtesy of The Advertising Archives.

Images on pages 7, 13, 25, 43, 63, 87, 99, 121, 133, 140
reproduced courtesy of Typhoon International Ltd
www.typhooneurope.com. Typhoon is widely recognized
as the first choice for stylish, innovative, and unique
cookware products.

Image on front of jacket reproduced courtesy of The
Advertising Archives; back jacket photograph by Diana
Miller; jacket background pattern taken from Flower
Mist plate produced for Midwinter by Jessie Tait in
1956. "Midwinter" is a registered trademark of Josiah
Wedgwood & Sons Ltd.